Hollering Sun

Nancy Wood

Photographs by
Myron Wood

Simon and Schuster
New York

For Richard

Nancy Wood

To my friends there

Myron Wood

The thoughts presented in this book are those of the Taos Indians. They were passed on over a period of ten years to the author, who wrote them down as poems, aphorisms and sayings. From her long friendship with these people has come a unique opportunity to capture the Indian way of looking at life. Except for the legends, the philosophy is universal.

The place seems right for the Taos Indians. Buffalo clouds behind a mountain that rises straight up from a sun-baked plain. The stark and lonely valley pressed flat by glaciers, with a gash running down the middle of it. The Spanish named it Rio Grande. The Indians didn't name it anything.

The sun locks the land in dryness, cracks it open and seals it up. In the heat and the light, the land shimmers and dissolves along the horizon. There is no detail, only the bold shapes of mesas and mountains, painted in the rich colors of the southwest. Burnt colors. Like an Indian's skin or his saddle or his horse. The land is big. From the mountain looking west there seems no end to it. It rolls on past the river and past the mesas, immense and silent, with the wind forever blowing over it.

The village has burst from the land. It is made of the earth itself, with doors the color of the sky. Piñon smoke hangs over the plaza, even in summer. In winter, when the creek that separates the two pueblos, or villages, is frozen solid, the smoke has the effect of a curtain. Here is a world which is and never was. Anachronistic. Enduring. Spun out of the imagination, verified by history. No wonder it's difficult to sort out what really is and really isn't. Too much hokum, says the white man. Too much white man, says the Indian.

The white man has to know about true beginnings. He has his theories on how the Taos got to that particular spot in New Mexico long before it was New Mexico or the United States or had any particular name at all. He says maybe the Taos descended from the Mayas who fled north, or from the aborigines who moved south after crossing the Bering Straits. He says maybe the Taos spun off from the Chinese when a tumbling junk washed up on the Pacific shore. So reads Chinese history.

The Indian prefers to think that the Chinese came from him. He believes that his were the first people upon the earth. So goes his story.

Far up on Taos Mountain lies a body of water the Taos call Blue Lake. A lake of the spirits. A lake where the dead go. A lake where the thoughts of the living come to rest. A lake that is the source of all life. A lake from which they rose as a people before the time of history, almost before the time of legends. Once risen, they wandered south and at Abiquiu met other Indians who taught them how to live. They built a pueblo at Ojo Caliente and long years passed. But something moved them south, to the Black Mountains, perhaps in Arizona. They were happy—these children of the sun. Perhaps century melted into century or decade into decade. The Indian doesn't much care to count time except by seasons and moons and harvests and hunts. What is a man's lifetime, he will say, except so many steps upon the earth? Or as a link between generations? Or for the purpose of carrying the thread of life across mountains and mesas and deserts, down through so many harvests that he cannot count them all? Time passed at the Black Mountains until perhaps there was a sickness or a drought or a famine. The Indian doesn't much care about details of departure either. This time they went north, marching slowly, for they had by then large numbers of domesticated turkeys, which they drove before them. Stopping on the way, they built a new pueblo and lived for a generation or more. Long enough to keep the thread running. Long enough to leave their footprints in the dust.

Traveling north again, the Indians came to a place of food and water. Here part of the tribe decided to stay, and they became the Picuris. The others came on into Rio Grande valley and lived first over beyond Llano on a beautiful hilltop which, commanding a wide view, gave them ample time to prepare when enemies approached. Where does the legend end? Where do facts begin? The ruins of home walls are still there at Llano. And the circle of an early kiva has yet another wall within it, suggesting that the Indians returned to rebuild the home that their ancestors, for some unknown reason, had left. Other pueblo walls, leveled but not quite lost, suggest a journey which mysteriously circled the valley around to the west by Cordova, then flung north. An anthropological question mark. An archaeological puzzle. An Indian nonfact of life.

Perhaps it was there, among the rocks and dry places and the trees growing short and scrawny, that their chief boy, chosen at first in a spirit of fun, grew to manhood and dominated the tribe so that when he ordered once again a migration, the Indians obeyed. Some there were who would not follow but later made their way to the site of their present home and became the Isleta tribe. The main body of Indians, however, followed their great chief. Above them in the brittle sunlight, an eagle wheeled and turned them south again, dropping two feathers near a soaring, rockbound peak. "Here," commanded the eagle, "you shall build two pueblos." Then he lifted his great wings and was lost in endless sky.

Thus it was that the Taos Indians began to build their homes of many stories and their underground kivas, and around it all they put a wall. For materials they used mud and straw and manure, all mixed together and formed into bricks, which dried for many days in the sun. The houses were good houses and lasted a long time, patched now and then with more adobe, added to now and then, until a century or so ago the pueblo reached its present size—big enough to house about 1,400 people in apartment-style living. But without the accommodations.

So came the Taos Indians into the valley seven hundred years ago. Or maybe a thousand. Or maybe two thousand years have swung their way into the silent past. Clues lie in the pueblo garbage dump, in the fields and plazas, in the walls of the houses. The white man has asked permission to dig, to probe, to find out the facts. The <u>facts</u>? To the Taos, the facts are that his corn grows, his feet dance, his voice sings, his land endures. When and where he came from do not require facts. An eagle will do. Or a giant. Or God spreading out his fingers so that all the tribes of the world fall through. Except Taos. Which stays in the palm of God's hand. What more do you need? And the white man may <u>not</u> dig in the garbage dump. Let him ask questions to satisfy a curiosity that the Indian does not possess. Or envy. Let the white man ask a question, and the Taos will give him ten different answers. Why? Because he likes it, says the Indian. Consider the word <u>Taos</u>, for instance. What does it <u>mean</u>, asks the white man?

Some will tell you they don't know. Some will say it means "A Gateway to Heaven" or "The Place from Which Comes Everything Good." Another Taos version is that long, long ago they had a great chief named Ta-oo and among their many gods was one Aosi, the contraction of which produced <u>Taos</u>. But the white man, desperately trying to link the Indians to the Chinese, points out the great philosopher Lao-tze once wrote a treatise called "Tao-Feh-King." The word <u>Tao</u> means in Chinese "the way" or "the right way" and was in use long before the days of Lao-tze. And there <u>is</u> a marked similarity between the Tewa speech of the Taos and that of the Chinese. One archaeologist excitedly wrote that "Tewa speech is excessively nasal and much broken by the glottal stop. Like Chinese, it makes use of 'tones.' There are forty-five distinct individual sounds; twelve of these sounds are vowels and may be long or short." <u>Glottal stop</u>? You might as well talk to the Taos about a hypotenuse.

All he will say about his language is that "nobody ever bothered us about it"—which, freely translated, means "White man mind your business." There is no alphabet, no written word. It drives the scientists to despair, and they write down what the Tewa language <u>sounds</u>

like. But the Taos merely shrugs and says it's Picuris. Crude and clearly inferior. Why should language be written down anyway? Do you bottle the wind?

For a long time the "savages" called Taos lived as all savages did before the white man came along to "improve" them. They could neither read nor write; they neither worked for wages nor were motivated by profit. All they had was their land and their gods and each other. A simplistic faith that good was rewarded and evil punished, that all things were a part of nature and therefore part of God. Praise be to the rock and the insects, to the birds and the furred creatures, to the Father Sun and the Mother Earth. Praise be to life itself, the greatest of all gifts. All men are brothers and we do not kill our brothers except when our brothers kill us. The Comanches and the Apaches and the Utes.

So it was for half a dozen centuries, more or less. Indians defending themselves against Indians. Then a curious thing happened.

When the first Spaniards came across the plains in 1541 there seems to have been one more adventurous than the others. He came riding ahead with his burro. The Indians had never seen such an animal nor such a man. They believed this was a sort of elk bringing into their midst a god or a spirit. Then followed others of these strangers with their bright dress, glittering spears and breastplates. The Indians came out to meet them. Neither could understand the other. Sign language helped Coronado's Captain Alvarado in 1540 and Barrionuevo some months later. They "left the province" in peace, and for the next half century the old men told tales to their children of a strange people who came and went away and never returned.

But not for long. In 1598 another group of these people came over the trail from Picuris, led by Oñate, who brought along his priests. Again the Indians greeted the strangers in a friendly manner and watched long-robed friars move among the soldiers quietly and say strange words when they lifted a small crossed stick. They too had a cross symbol sacred to them and so they submitted to baptism as part of "good medicine."

When the first church was to be built, the friars had the Indians drag or carry on their shoulders great rocks for the foundation of the building. Recalcitrant Indians felt the whip of their friar masters. The Indian began to smolder under indignities, yet continued to be baptized until, by 1628, the monk Benavides reported triumphantly to his Spanish king that there were 2,500 baptized souls in Taos. By 1650, another church was to be built, but the Indians had not forgotten the experience their fathers had had with the heavy rocks, or the lashings for lagging behind. The Taos men began to meet secretly in their kivas to discuss whether they should try to get rid of the Spaniards, priest and all. Deer skins were procured, and the village scribe wrote the picture message which all Indians would understand, asking them to join in revolt. But it was not until 1676 that Popé, the San Juan shaman (medicine man) with a police court record, decided that Taos Pueblo was the place for him to come and plot against the Spaniards. The Taos received him cordially and listened attentively.

He reminded them that the Pueblo Indians had met the Spanish in peace and, in response to Spanish professions of friendship, had given food and shelter as proof of their own. But the friendship soon withered; Spanish garrisons collected tribute levied on the Indians, extorted for each Spanish soldier an encomienda of Indian land with Indian serfs to work it, and tried to suppress the Indian religion. Indian protests were put down with violence, the Indian leaders hanged, and the rank and file whipped and imprisoned, or sent as slaves to Spanish mines in Mexico.

So much for the savages, reasoned the Spaniards.

So much for the Spaniards, reasoned the Indians.

Under Pópe's leadership, the Indians joined together an alliance of more than sixty pueblos, united on so broad a scale for the first and last time in history. Even the Apaches and the Navajos joined the alliance. The revolt was planned and kept in strictest secrecy throughout four years of preparation for war, over a territory covering 40,000 square miles of mountains and desert, among tribes of many different languages and customs, directed toward a simultaneous uprising at dawn on a given day. A cord of yucca, knotted to tell the number of days to pass before war was waged against the Spaniards, was sent by swiftest runners to all the pueblos.

Three days early the fury broke. Taos Indians and others killed all they could about the pueblo and swept southward to surround Santa Fe. The Spaniards were driven all the way across the Rio Grande into Mexico, about 500 miles away, and the only whites left in what is now New Mexico were kept as slaves. When, twelve years later, Don Diego de Vargas led the Spanish back, they came as settlers; they accepted the Indian religion and sought cooperation instead of slavery. Popé had died and the intertribal council had no heart for further war.

For almost 250 years, until 1847, the Taos did no more revolting. The unrest began in 1836 when the Mexican president appointed Coronel Albino Pérez—a veritable campesino—as territorial governor of New Mexico. The appointment angered the leaders of New Mexican society, who were used to having one of their own elite—a Baca or a Chavez or an Armijo—as governor. They soon contrived to incite an uprising against new taxes sponsored by Governor Pérez. Northern New Mexico had grievances of long standing against the territorial government, and revolt was easily stirred up.

The Taos Indians joined forces with the Spaniards in a rebel army which soon drove off the beleaguered Governor Pérez, who was given no support whatsoever by the aristocrats of Santa Fe and Albuquerque. The leaders of the rebel army then called together a general assembly, which elected an even stranger choice as governor —José Gonzales, a Taos Indian. Revolt followed revolt—a crazy quilt of power struggles, culture shocks and zany leadership. First to fall was Gonzales, driven off by Manuel Armijo, who was driven off by General Stephen W. Kearny's Army of the West that had invaded New Mexico and arrived in Santa Fe virtually unopposed. Charles Bent was installed as the first territorial governor of New Mexico, and the new regime rocked unsteadily on its way.

The Spaniards and the Indians, meanwhile, plotted to wrest the territory away from the United States. In 1847, Mexicans and Indians joined in the murder of Governor Bent and his son at the town of Taos, five miles south of the pueblo. Troops were sent to the pueblo and stormed the old church where the Indians huddled. The church was shelled, and all uprising Indians who were not killed on the spot were hanged. However, one old Indian who survived told of being in the fight and said, "Indian, Indian, he like prairie dog." Pawing the air, he tried to show how the Taos in their fight made frantic efforts to dig themselves into the adobe walls of the church.

So much for group violence at the pueblo. From then on the cowed Indians led a peaceful coexistence with the Spaniards and the white man, trusting neither. They would not fight and go the way of the Sioux, the Utes, the Cheyennes, the Apaches, the Comanches. Wiped out, exiled, humiliated, ripped from the land and therefore from life. Pride is a curious emotion with the Taos. He saves it for things that count. Like making the most of the land he has left—which just happens to be the most productive, beautiful and pristine of any Indian reservation. Like waging a different kind of war with the government, relying on patience, tact and an abiding faith in his own gods and his own people rather than an abiding faith in weapons, treaties or bureaucrats. And so, against unbelievable odds and against precedents which always take the land away from the Indian and give it to the white man forever, the Taos went about regaining ownership of Blue Lake. A lake of the spirits. A lake where the dead go. A lake where the thoughts of the living come to rest. A lake that is the source of all life. A lake from which they rose as a people before the time of history, almost before the time of legends. A lake added to the public domain by Teddy Roosevelt in 1906. He included it among 130,000 acres of land grabbed from the Taos and made part of a 1.5-million-acre national forest named for celebrated Indian killer Kit Carson. The Taos, naturally, were never consulted. They were, however, allowed by the Forest Service to continue to come to their sacred lake to conduct religious services. At the same time, the Forest Service also encouraged campers and tourists to visit Blue Lake. A scenic attraction. Ideal for recreation. The Land of Many Abuses. After all, who needs a 130,000-acre church? What do they do with it? Oh, they might pray to a rock. Or an eagle. Or a tree. Or maybe to the clouds. Or to the lake itself. They call all those things "shrines" and say they are sacred. Sacred? What is sacred about a piece of land that ought to have a privy on it? That way, more tourists could come.

In 1933 Congress tried to placate the indignant Indians by passing legislation that gave them a fifty-year special-use permit, restricting the area to their "use and benefit." It also said that the general public, other than Forest Service personnel, was not to use the area without permission from the Indians and the forest supervisor. But that "solution" failed when the Forest Service continued to allow public recreation in the area without consulting the Indians. Although no more than ninety non-Indians ever invaded the area in a single year, the Taos insisted that _any_ intrusion meant they did not have exclusive rights to the site. No religious freedom, they said. Wasn't that guaranteed by the Bill of Rights to _all_ citizens, even Indians? No. In this case, we will give you a Bill of Wrongs, supplemented by a Bill of Goods. We will pay you good cash money for Blue Lake.

In 1965 the Indian Claims Commission ruled that the Taos had been unjustly deprived of their property. But the I.C.C., operated by the Bureau of Indian Affairs, was not authorized to restore Blue Lake to its owners. In lieu of restoration, the I.C.C. recommended that the Indians be given financial compensation for their loss. All 130,000 acres. At 1906 prices.

The Indians rejected the offer just as they did in 1924, when they were offered several hundred thousand dollars by the federally sponsored Pueblo Lands Commission. Other pueblos sold off their land. Why not the Taos?

> Do you know how to speak to the land, my brother?
> Do you listen to what it tells you?
> Can you take from it no more than what you need?
> Can you keep its secrets to yourself?
> Sell the land, my brother?
> You might as well sell
> The sun, the moon, the stars.

All the Taos Indian really wanted was a compromise. Forty-eight thousand acres, including Blue Lake. Delivered back to him by the United States government at its earliest convenience. The Taos learned English. They learned about land-title documents, lobbying in Congress, raising money to pay for trips to Washington, and the phrases of justice which appeal to a nation and a Congress aware of guilt. The Indians were adamant. After three years of intense pressure, the House of Representatives gave in—unanimously. In the Senate, it was a different story. New Mexico's very own Senator Clinton P. Anderson was against it. He said that he was afraid that heeding the Taos demand would lead to the "breakup of forest preserves," because other Indian groups would demand passage of similar special-interest legislation. They might even demand compensation for Manhattan Island. Too bad, said the Taos. We want our land. And they went about convincing everyone that was exactly what they should have.

In December, 1970, the sixty-four-year-old battle came to an end. The United States Senate voted 70 to 12 to give Blue Lake back to the Indians.

In Taos, it was Quiet Time, the Indians' period of introspection and contemplation, the time when all activity ceases and nothing is celebrated. Not even the greatest victory of a tribe perhaps two thousand years old. The church bell rang briefly. A tear rolled down the cheek of one old man in the plaza. That was all. The Taos were not surprised, just thankful. But they could not interrupt their Quiet Time to show it. There would be a time to rejoice in a place where time does not matter, a place that is a remnant of a land that was very big and very good. A remnant plundered by the Spanish, exploited by the Anglos, commercialized by itself.

And yet it lives. Lives after more than forty similar pueblos along the Rio Grande have disappeared into history and the remaining seventeen are slowly but surely being swallowed up by civilization.

Civilization. A word the Taos Indian despises—and lives with. A word he knows spells doom if such "improvements" as electricity and paved roads are allowed into his domain. A word that has meant his education, his vote, his automobile, and for some, a permanent drifting away from the old ways.

Civilization. Improvement. Change. Authorization. Compensation. Forked tongue. Tensions from within. Pressures from without. The Catholic faith superimposed upon their own religion when the Spaniards came in the sixteenth century to convert them to Christianity. So what is Christianity, they ask, except another celebration of life?

In summer the wind blows across the plaza of the Taos Pueblo and tourists come to stare at the five-story, adobe-mud buildings which seem to have sprung from the earth. Blanket-wrapped Indian men stand motionless against the adobe wall which surrounds the pueblo, or stand on their roof, faces to the sun. Some of them move restlessly out into the the fields, on foot, on horseback, in wagons, and pickup trucks.

In the plaza there are paradoxes. Curio shops and fat adobe ovens. Animal skins stretched out to dry. The wash blowing from clotheslines. The sound of battery-operated television sets and the sound of a beating drum. The heady fragrance of the piñon fires and the stench of the internal-combustion engine. Indians climb down wooden ladders—there are no stairs anywhere—wrapped in blankets from J. C. Penney's. Women in shawls carry water in buckets from the stream while children play with toy pistols and model rockets.

They love to dance, these Indians, and they beat their drums and sing the soft, melodious words of the Tewa language. There is the Turtle Dance and the Deer Dance, the Buffalo Dance and the Corn Dance. The Indians are in feathered headdresses, beaded moccasins, costumes made of deerskin, faces painted with pigments dug out of the mountain at Questa. The tourists can watch the dances and sense that here is something genuine. But where is the rest of it? Where is the Indian mystique they have come so far to find? The sudden understanding of why fourteen hundred Indians are all crammed into a dusty village with neither plumbing nor electricity. The essence. The philosophy. The nobility. Where is it? Not to be found in a one-hour visit. Nor do the tourist guides nor the tomes by sociologists and anthropologists offer a clue as to what the Taos Indian really is.

Back in the town of Taos five miles away, there are often enough disheveled Indians wandering the streets to reinforce the white man's belief that Indians are dirty, drunk, lazy, and the sooner they become assimilated into the American culture the better off they'll be. Enough for the average American tourist. And the Indian on the corner charges a dollar for you to take his picture. Outrageous exploitation of the white man.

The Taos Indian reveals nothing. He does not care if the white man understands him or not. He does not fear the world or believe it can do him much good either. He blames it for much of his misfortune. Rain does not fall on Taos Pueblo the way it used to, because the flight pattern of the daily jets cuts right through the rain clouds. The failure of his crops, the earthquakes and the drought are due to the fact that man has gone to the moon. And as the world continues its mad, mindless pursuits, the Taos say that in the end the world will literally come to their doorstep and the Indians will teach them how to live. Practical things. Like growing food and hunting animals. And how to cook a porcupine. Like taking care of the land. The white man calls it ecology. The Taos calls it a way of life. And he's known it from the beginning. He goes his way, serenely, waiting for the world to catch up.

Unlike the Navajo, the Taos does not write down his thoughts. His poetry is in his soul. Unlike most of his Indian brothers, the best of his land still remains in his hands. He has mountains, streams, fields, canyons, meadows, forests, and now his sacred Blue Lake, as essential to him as his breath. What makes the Taos unique is his land, the vastness and the beauty of it, the variety and power of it. What makes him unique is his sprawling, architecturally magnificent dwelling place. What makes him unique is his unity with his tribesmen, a unity which includes a willingness to suffer tyranny gladly in order to preserve the rights and obligations of his people. Between the human soul and the earth he stands, often noble and often wise, a paradox of universality and isolation.

All as it was in this place timeless.
All as it was between the human soul and the earth
For there is no difference between
The life of a man and the life
Of all growing things.
Who is to say if a man
Shall not be a tree instead?
We pray to all of nature and do it no harm.
These are our brothers
All men and all animals and all trees.
Some part of ourselves
Is in earth and sky and everywhere.
It shall continue
As long as nature follows its own purpose.
It shall continue
As long as we know what we are doing here.

When God made the earth he held all the people of the world in his hand. And they slipped through his fingers and became the tribes of the earth. But God held the tribe of Taos in the palm of his hand, for these people were the center of the earth and God set them down carefully.

When it came time for the tribe of Taos to know the earth and to become part of nature, a giant set them in the mountain. The giant still walks the mountain and is not seen by anyone. But each boy of Taos, when he reaches a certain age, must go to the mountain alone, and he must stay there until he finds the footprint of the giant. And when this happens he may begin to call himself a man.

A long time ago the Coyote brought the buffalo to Taos from the faraway plains of the rising sun. The buffalo went dancing while Coyote sang, and the buffalo danced to the Coyote's singing all the way to Taos. Then Coyote gave the buffalo to Big Earring People and to Day People and to Ax Chief and told them the buffalo would be theirs and to take part in the dance with the first man. And so Coyote went back to his home in the buffalo country, and the people began to dance with the buffalo and are still dancing.

From the edge of the hole in the sky
In the land of the thunder birds,
The eagle looked down and saw
The pueblo of the people who never were
And never will be.
He flew through the hole in the sky
To the pueblo of the people who never were
And never will be.
He was too happy there.
When the eagle returned to the land of the thunder birds
He had no feathers and so he fell down to the earth
As a rock who could never tell of the happiness
At the pueblo of the people who never were
And never will be.

The journey of the raindrop began in a cloud that wished to cry.
The journey of the raindrop continued on the wing of a butterfly.
The raindrop fell through the air blown by a wind from the west.
The raindrop was caught by a tree which gave it branch to branch.
The raindrop stood alone at the end of a leaf and cried to a star.
The raindrop fell to the earth and went with the river that roars.
The journey of the raindrop will not end until the Great Spirit kills the sea.

A tear fell from the eye of the Blue Corn mother, fell to the earth that was bare. The tear of the Blue Corn mother stayed in the earth a long time, stayed in the earth and waited for the walking rain to come. Then the tear of the Blue Corn mother grew to the flower of fire and burns in the wind to this day.

Earth woman with hands
That shape the bread of time.
Earth woman with
Pumpkin-seed earrings and
Bracelets of wild plum.
Your house is made of summer.
Your children are the crops
Of all good seasons
Growing strong
In the house of earth woman
Who weaves the thread of life.

An ant came out
Of his home in the ant hill
And slept in the winter sun.
The sky grew dark
As the little ant slept
And a snowflake fell from the sky
Fell and broke the little ant's foot
So soft did it fall from the sky.

The hawk is not a plain fly-catching bird.
The hawk is not a magpie-teasing bird.
The hawk is a lonely hunter bird.
It has one poison feather in its wing with which to kill its prey.

The snake is a ribbon of riches sliding over cracked earth wise.
The snake cannot come in my house nor can I touch its ribbon of riches.
Evil will come to me if I do.
I pray to the snake to stay away.

All day long the cricket waits to sing
Until at last the darkness gives him music
For his voice to follow through the night.
He sings to the bat and to the owl
To the field mouse and to the earthworm.
He wakes the morning birds and then he goes to sleep.

The Old Man called to his sons, called them
Eagle Dances and Elk Talk, Deer Chief and Antelope Water.
The Old Man called to his daughters, called them
Corn Appears and Flower-go-Pluck, For Her Flower Dances
and For Her Lake Dances.
The Old Man said to them, consider the sun
Which travels every day and does not tire.
We should be like the sun.
We should not tire.
We should not complain.
We should not give up simply because it is dark.

For us it is not bad luck to whistle in the night like a bear or an elk or an owl. For us whistling in the night is to answer our sleeping brothers.

It is bad luck for a man to eat from a cracked plate or drink from a cracked cup. If he does, then he will be killed in war or even if just one enemy falls upon him in the village in the night.

If I hunger after the peacock's beauty, the peacock shall bring me death. I pray to the peacock to keep its beauty to itself.

The deer live at the deer yawn and have a way of dressing their children with white spots. The Deer woman does this by shutting her children in a room and closing all the holes and the door and setting corncobs on fire in the fireplace. The little deer run into the burning corncobs and that is how they get their spots.

The coyote lived at sun house,
The buffalo at people creek;
The mountain sheep lived in the Great White Mountain,
The Gopher Old Woman lived at cottonwood tree windfall.
But I lived at the Edge-of-the-grass near the Mountain-of-White-Earth.
I lived where the deer were living.
I lived like a deer and spoke like a deer
For many days.
Then I returned to my people as a man of the deer.

Blue lake of life from which flows everything good.
We rejoice with the spirits beneath your waters.
The lake and the earth and the sky
Are all around us.
The voices of many gods
Are all within us.
We are now as one with rock and tree
As one with eagle and crow
As one with deer and coyote
As one with all things
That have been placed here by the Great Spirit.
The sun that shines upon us
The wind that wipes our faces clean of fear
The stars that guide us on this journey
To our blue lake of life
We rejoice with you.
In beauty it is begun.
In beauty it is begun.
In peace it is finished.
In peace it shall never end.

A rainbow is just
The great spirit painting
A circle around the earth.
The half that belongs
In my sky
Is made with colors
Of my life.
The half that belongs
Below the earth
Is made with colors
Of my death.

The twelfth moon came orange from the other side of the earth. And one star dropped from the sky because there was not room for both. The star became the eyes of a man who could not see. The moon watched over the earth and fell into the mountain when it was time for the sun to begin.

Who can say if the corn will be good or not? The Yellow Corn mother knows. We listen. We hear the Yellow Corn mother say touch the earth with your feet and let your singing be heard by the sun. Then we dance for the good corn of the Yellow Corn mother. The bad corn is danced away by our feet and goes to the place of dryness and dead winds.

THE VILLAGE

It is the quiet time of winter when all of nature sleeps, when the water is not flowing and the grass is not growing and the sun is giving only half itself to the day.

The dust is blowing on the mountain. The dust is the mountain growing. The mountain heals itself just like man if you give it time to rest.

Do not move the rock or anything placed in its place by God. Not a leaf from a tree nor a bird from its nest nor a spider's silver thread. These things will fall soon enough in their time.

The earth has roots, and the roots belong to the soil. If you cut a hole in the soil you have damaged the earth. You must therefore be certain it is necessary.

It is our quiet time.
We do not speak because the voices are within us.
It is our quiet time.
We do not walk, because the earth is all within us.
It is our quiet time.
We do not dance, because the music has lifted us to a place where the spirit is.
It is our quiet time.
We rest with all of nature. We wake when the seven sisters wake. We greet them
in the sky over the opening of the kiva.

One man must always rise in the dark and go to the mountain to greet the sun at dawn. If man were not to do this, the sun would not rise.

Pieces of sun on the lake of my spirits; pieces of sun on waters of eagle and hawk; pieces of sun lie broken on the waters of the lake from which come the voice to all my singing, the eyes to all my beauty, the peace to all my longing.

Above all is the long-living spirit which is the thread from generation to generation, as long as the land we live on is everlasting and our children have a place to lie down.

We shall live together;
We shall walk with you;
We shall find in each new day what hides inside of you.
We shall wait together;
We shall see the day when we go hand in hand
To the fire in the mountain,
To the water in the sand.

All as it was, peace.
All as it was, love.
All as it was, beauty.
All as it was, order.
All as it was, in exactly the right place.
This place of the sun trail
The buffalo-grass plain
The hummingbird spring
The grass hat
The fog mesa
And the Big House in the lake where good spirits live.
This place of my people
This place of my grandsons still unborn.
Everything good is to be found here.
Everything good is to be kept here.

What, my son, does your blanket mean?
And how shall you wear it as the man you must become?
It shall give you warmth of flesh.
It shall protect you from evil spirits.
But most of all
It shall be your vow
To keep the promise of your ancestors
That your village shall never die.

Let us move evenly together.
Let us stand as one.
Let evil be cast from us.
Let no man cry for himself
Or listen to those without faces.
Let us move evenly together.
Let us walk as tall trees.
Let fear be crushed within us.
Let no man speak for himself
Or give secrets to those without blood.

My brother the star, my mother the earth, my father the sun, my sister the moon, to my life give beauty, to my body give strength, to my corn give goodness, to my house give peace, to my spirit give truth, to my elders give wisdom.

Oh my gentle village fierce
Oh my powerful people weak
Oh my fertile fields so dry
Oh my peaceful house disturbed
We must pray for strength.
We must pray to come together
Pray to the weeping earth
Pray to the trembling waters
And to the wandering rain.
We must pray to the whispering moon
Pray to the tiptoeing stars
And to the hollering sun.

This was our land.
The land that the mountain needed in order
To rise in majesty.
The land that my people needed in order
To roam its secrets in reverence.
This land was the land
Of our great waters
The beating heart of nature flowing through time
That we could not remember.
This was our land.
The land that provided everything good for my people.
The land was always our land
And the sun set upon it
The rain washed it
And the fire was kind in its fury.
It was so for all time.
Then the land was taken from us.
It is your land.
Do you know how to speak to the land, my brother?
Do you listen to what it tells you?
Can you take from it no more than what you need?
Can you keep its secrets to yourself?
Sell the land, my brother?
You might as well sell
The sun, the moon, the stars.

The world out there called to my son,
And so he went to see if it was a good world.
He went to hear its music.
He went because he had to.
A long time passed and then my son returned.
He said the world out there is like
The porcupine that fights with the turtle
Or like fire that has fallen into water.
There is no music either.

I went to learn how the white man lives.
I went to learn if he's free.
I went to learn the white man's ways
But I found them a stranger to me.
Shall I teach you, my brother?
Shall I teach you to live and to see?
Shall I teach you the Indian way?
Listen, my brother.
My words are those of dead generations
And of generations still to be.
My words I give to you.
The meaning is for you to find.

You tell us that times are changing.
You say that we do not know
The times in which we live.
We say to you that this time is like any other time
If a man's feet are on the ground
And his heart is in the right place
And he does not try to make
The eagle into an airplane.

How should I live?
Among my people a small voice?
In your world silent?
Among my people there is no horizon.
In your world I have seen
The universe contained in glass.

What is there for me when I have finished planting?
What is there for me at the end of the row I must hoe?
What is there for me when the harvest is over?
Better corn.
That is all.

The sun in late afternoon gives life to all the rocks and dry places.

How do I know it is spring? When in the night the ice on the creek breaks and my sleep breaks also.

My father's face is in the rock on the mountain; the rock of many faces and many fathers; the rock to which I turn and all sons turn to see the face of all our fathers on the mountain.

The voice of my fathers is on the wind and my voice also when it becomes strong for only my sons to hear and keep on hearing after I am gone.

To fly higher than the eagle, to run faster than the deer, to swim as freely as the fish, to have the cunning of the coyote and the sleekness of the lion—this is to possess the spirit that sings in the wind and cries in the fire, the spirit that shall never leave my home.

My horse took me down the life-giving road
Drawing his breath as he went
His breath of strong spirit
His breath of power to plow and to pull.
But now he is old
And his breath is of feathers and corn.
I add to his breath
The breath of my own
And pray to his old age of riches.

Every morning I walk into the tent of the mountain. I stand secure. I am in peace. The wind comes. This is the breath of the mountain telling me the path to take.

I am gone and am going to the mountain so that I may see the lightning break the sky in two and rain come to heal it up again.

I come to the place where I have stepped before. The wind blows my steps away in the dust. The steps of all who walk here go with the wind and walk with the sky.

Up here is quiet. My feet are quiet. My hands are quiet. My eyes are also quiet. They see a bird flying quiet, a tree blowing quiet, a moon rising quiet. Only my soul is not quiet. My soul does not rest until the corn is planted.

There is an eagle in me
and a spotted bird
hurrying corn to grow.
The eagle flies to the
mountains of my dreams, flies
to the corners of my distant hopes.
But the spotted bird
stands among the cornstalks
telling me to hoe.

My hands are the tools of my soul.
They make the drum, the bow, the
flute, and stretch the skin of the
deer. They work the earth and
care for the sheep and plant the
corn. They greet my homeland
each morning that I awake.

I went to kill the deer
Deep in the forest where
The heart of the mountain beats
For all who live there.
An eagle saw me coming and
Flew down to the home of the deer
And told him that
A hunter came to kill.
The deer went with the eagle
Into the heart of the mountain
Safe from me who did not hear
The heart of the mountain beating.

When trouble comes to me
I have to go and dance.
I dance until the dust receives my trouble.
The dust takes my trouble to the mountain.
The mountain grows with the dust of trouble.
The place for my trouble to be.

My feet touch earth and dance to the drums
which are in my heart as well. If my feet do not
touch earth the dance will not be good. And
the music in my heart will all be still.

To kill the eagle is
To kill the peace
Which rests in the hearts
Of men and villages.
To kill the eagle is
To kill the strength
Of warriors and wise men.
To kill the eagle is
To kill the freedom
That nature gives
To every living thing.
What should be is
The eagle flying
As shadow to the sun
And chieftain to the sky.

My help is in the mountain
Where I take myself to heal
The earthly wounds
That people give to me.
I find a rock with sun on it
And a stream where the water runs gentle
And the trees which one by one give me company.
So must I stay for a long time
Until I have grown from the rock
And the stream is running through me
And I cannot tell myself from one tall tree.
Then I know that nothing touches me
Nor makes me run away.
My help is in the mountain
That I take away with me.

Earth cure me. Earth receive my woe. Rock
strengthen me. Rock receive my weakness. Rain
wash my sadness away. Rain receive my doubt.
Sun make sweet my song. Sun receive the anger
from my heart.

Mountain of discontent.
Mountain of talking gods
And cold fire.
Mountain of dry bones
And silent drums
I feed on your ashes
I cry to your empty womb.
Where is your comfort
In this time for staying still?

I lay on the rock in the stream
long enough so that what was
not good in me washed down
and away, gone from my body
forever.

Time takes me on its wing
and I travel to the sun
And am consumed by fire.
Time takes me on its wing
and I travel to the river
And am drowned in water.
Time takes me on its wing
and I travel into the earth
And am a mountain not yet risen.
Each place that I go

Others have gone before me.
That is why
The sun dances
The wind weeps
The river leaps
And the earth sings.
Neither the sun nor the wind
The river nor the earth
Did these things
Before man was placed in the world
To believe it.

Fire fire of the first world
giving man his heat,
Air air of the second world
giving man his breath,
Water water of the third world
giving man his life stream,
Earth earth of the fourth world
giving man himself.
I am a turtle crawling
out of the water upon
dry land at dawn
To begin the dance of life.

Leaf that falls yellow from a learning tree
Leaf that dances along with me
Gathering other yellow leaves until
We are all dancing to please the hollering sun
To the music of the leaf-eating wind
That blows autumn into the mouth of winter.

The rain walked with long legs
Across the cracked-earth mesa
And the floor of the sky
Where the corn was dying.
The walking rain
Healed up the cracked-earth mesa
And wept on the floor of the sky
Until the corn stalks grew
Straight and tall enough to reach
The feet of the walking rain.

Come you Four Winds!
Come here and stand in four places.
Come you Four Winds!
Turn this child to the east
Turn this child to the south
Turn this child to the west
Turn this child to the north
Turn this child to the east.
Turned by the Four Winds
This child goes where the four hills of life
And the Four Winds are standing.
There into the midst of the Winds does he go.
By many roads does he travel.
All roads are the same if they lead to the light,
If they lead to the four hills of life.

I am old now and covered with my life.

The drum is broken.
The hoe is still.
We have cheated the sun
And betrayed the universe.
This then is how we die.

What I am I must become.
What I see I must try to find.
What I hear I must play music to.
What I touch I must leave alone
And turn then to all reflections of myself
In trees and sacred things
That nature gives to me.

Never shall I leave the places that I love;
Never shall they go from my heart
Even though my eyes
Are somewhere else.

I have killed the deer.
I have crushed the grasshopper
And the plants he feeds upon.
I have cut through the heart
Of trees growing old and straight.
I have taken fish from water
And birds from the sky.
In my life I have needed death
So that my life can be.
When I die I must give life
To what has nourished me.
The earth receives my body
And gives it to the plants
And to the caterpillars
To the birds
And to the coyotes
Each in its own turn so that
The circle of life is never broken.